'Abdu'l-Bahá Loves Children

Nine Stories of 'Abdu'l-Bahá with Children

Written & Compiled by Alhan Rahimi

Illustrated by Kseniia Pavska

Copyright © 2021 by Alhan Rahimi

hello@alhanrahimi.com

ISBN: 978-1-990286-06-3 (Hardcover)

ISBN: 978-1-990286-05-6 (Paperback)

Written & compiled by Alhan Rahimi based on true historical events

Illustrations by Kseniia Pavska

Cover design by Kseniia Pavska & Mariam Jorjoliani

Source of quote on back cover:

("The Promulgation of Universal Peace: Talks Delivered by 'Abdu'l-Bahá during His Visit to the United States and Canada in 1912", 2nd. ed. (Wilmette: Bahá'í Publishing Trust, 1982), pp. 52–54) [147]

All rights reserved worldwide. No part of this book may be reproduced, distributed or transmitted in any form or by any means without the prior written permission of the author, except in the case of brief quotations embodied in critical reviews.

This book has been approved by the National Spiritual Assembly of the Bahá'ís of Canada.

'Abdu'l-Bahá walking up Haparsim Street with three kids eating sweets that 'Abdu'l-Bahá just gave them, c. 1920

'Abdu'l-Bahá says about children:

"The Kingdom of heaven is for such souls as these, for they are near to God. They have pure hearts. They have spiritual faces. The effect of the divine teachings is manifest in the perfect purity of their hearts... The hearts of all children are of the utmost purity. They are mirrors upon which no dust has fallen...

I give you my advice, and it is this: Train these children with divine exhortations. From their childhood instill in their hearts the love of God so they may manifest in their lives the fear of God and have confidence in the bestowals of God. Teach them to free themselves from human imperfections and to acquire the divine perfections latent in the heart of man... Therefore, make ye an effort in order that these children may be rightly trained and educated and that each of them may attain perfection in the world of humanity. Know ye the value of these children for they are all my children."[1]

'Abdu'l-Bahá with three children, 1912

This book is dedicated to the occasion of the centenary of the Ascension of 'Abdu'l-Bahá.

(1)
Two-Year-Old Shoghi Effendi

Shoghi Effendi was the eldest grandson of 'Abdu'l-Bahá and the Guardian of the Bahá'í Faith. Shoghi Effendi loved his grandfather and tried to make Him happy. There was a very special relationship between the two of them.

Shoghi Effendi at the time he became Guardian of the Bahá'í Faith, 1921

One day, when Shoghi Effendi was two years old, 'Abdu'l-Bahá was sitting in a room of 'Abdu'lláh Páshá's house and writing Tablets. The room was quiet, even though other family members were in there sipping their early morning tea.

Inner courtyard of the House of 'Abdu'lláh Páshá

After a prayer was said, Shoghi Effendi suddenly appeared at the doorway. He took off his shoes and walked into the room while focused on his grandfather. 'Abdu'l-Bahá looked back at him with such love that it was like a magnet, attracting him until he stood in front of Him. Everyone in the room was watching carefully to see what would happen next.

Next, two-year-old Shoghi Effendi waited a moment, picked up the hem of 'Abdu'l-Bahá's robe, placed it respectfully on his forehead, kissed it, and very gently put it back. All this time, he was gazing only at 'Abdu'l-Bahá's face. After that, he turned away and went off to play, just as any two-year-old would!

Full of energy, he sprinted up and down the stairs of the house. Once, 'Abdu'l-Bahá wrote a sentence on a used envelope to please him. The sentence was: "Shoghi Effendi is a wise man – but he runs about very much!"[2]

The First Tablet to Shoghi Effendi

'Abdu'l-Bahá wrote lots of letters to many people throughout His life. These letters are called Tablets. It was a great honor to receive one of those Tablets at that time. It felt like receiving a treasure!

When Shoghi Effendi was five years old, he also wanted to receive a Tablet from his grandfather, so he kept on begging 'Abdu'l-Bahá over and over to write something for him. Even though 'Abdu'l-Bahá was extremely busy with the matters of the Faith and had no time, He lovingly wrote the following to His grandson:

He is God!
O My Shoghi, I have no time to talk,
leave me alone!
You said "write" - I have written.
What else should be done?
Now is not the time for you to read and write,
it is the time for jumping about
and chanting "O My God!",
therefore memorize the prayers
of the Blessed Beauty and chant them that
I may hear them, because
there is no time for anything else.

I'm sure you can imagine how happy Shoghi Effendi was to receive a Tablet that he had been wanting for a while. He decided to follow what his grandfather asked him and memorize some of Bahá'u'lláh's prayers. He also wanted to make sure that 'Abdu'l-Bahá could hear him while he said those prayers, so he chanted them very loudly. The entire neighborhood could hear his voice. When some of his family members asked him to lower his voice, he replied, "The Master wrote to me to chant that He may hear me! I am doing my best!"

Yet he would not only say one prayer; rather, he would chant for hours every single day. He chanted prayers revealed by 'Abdu'l-Bahá for children. He also chanted prayers that 'Abdu'l-Bahá wrote after the ascension of Bahá'u'lláh. He was so touched by these that tears rolled down his little face.

However, family members were still a little annoyed by how loud his voice was. His parents talked to 'Abdu'l-Bahá about it and requested Him to stop him, but He asked his parents to let him chant prayers the way he liked. [3]

(3)
Shoghi Effendi Uses His Grandfather's Pen

One day, Shoghi Effendi entered his grandfather's room and tried to write with His pen. 'Abdu'l-Bahá, with all the love He had for him, drew him closer to Himself, tapped him on his shoulder, and told him, "Now is not the time to write, now is the time to play, you will write a lot in the future."

However, because of Shoghi Effendi's great love for learning, classes for children were started in 'Abdu'l-Bahá's home. [4]

'Abdu'l-Bahá in the Holy Land, c. 1920

(4)
Early Mornings

Rúhíyyih Khánum, the wife of Shoghi Effendi, wrote in her book, The Priceless Pearl, the following about his childhood:

"In those days of Shoghi Effendi's childhood it was the custom to rise about dawn and spend the first hour of the day in the Master's room, where prayers were said and the family all had breakfast with Him. The children sat on the floor, their legs folded under them... they would chant for 'Abdu'l-Bahá; there was no shouting or unseemly conduct. Breakfast consisted of tea, brewed on the bubbling Russian brass samovar and served in little crystal glasses, very hot and very sweet, pure wheat bread and goat's milk cheese... Shoghi Effendi was always the first to get up and be on time." [5]

Little Mary

Two-year old Mary lived in Montreal, Canada in 1912 when 'Abdu'l-Bahá visited that city. She was very happy that 'Abdu'l-Bahá stayed at their place for three days. He loved her very much and exclaimed, "She is the essence of sweetness!"

One day, 'Abdu'l-Bahá was resting after lunch on a couch at the foot of His bed. Mary's mother made sure everywhere was quiet in the house so that 'Abdu'l-Bahá could rest. She told her little daughter, Mary, not to wake 'Abdu'l-Bahá up. However, Mary loved 'Abdu'l-Bahá so much that she rushed into His room and raced up to Him. She opened His eyelids with her little fingers and said to him, "Wake up, 'Abdu'l-Bahá!"

Yet 'Abdu'l-Bahá didn't become upset with her. On the contrary, He held her and let her sleep in His arms as her head was pressed against His chest. Mary loved Him very much, so it was very hard for her to stay away from Him.

Mary was given the title of Amatu'l-Bahá Rúhíyyih Khánum by Shoghi Effendi after she was married to him.[6]

Amatu'l-Bahá Rúhíyyih Khánum (1910-2000)

(6)
The Two-Year-Old Granddaughter

'Abdu'l-Bahá loved children very much. One day, His two-year-old granddaughter was telling Him about her troubles, and he listened to her seriously.

At other times, when she chanted a prayer and forgot a word, He would gently remind her of it and then smile sweetly at her.[7]

'Abdu'l-Bahá in Dublin, New Hampshire, 26 July 1912

Leroy C. Ioas (1896-1965)

(7)
Leroy Ioas

This story took place in Chicago, America. There was once a young boy named Leroy Ioas. One day, he decided to buy some flowers for 'Abdu'l-Bahá, so he bought his own favourite kind – white carnations. But on the way to the hotel where 'Abdu'l-Bahá was going to give a talk, he changed his mind. His father wondered why Leroy had second thoughts. Leroy told him: "I come to the Master offering Him my heart, and I do not want Him to think I want any favours. He knows what's in a person's heart, and that is all I have to offer."

So instead, Leroy's father presented the white carnations to 'Abdu'l-Bahá, who became very delighted and put His face on them to enjoy their fragrance. While 'Abdu'l-Bahá was giving His talk, Leroy sat at His feet and stared at Him very attentively.

After 'Abdu'l-Bahá finished His talk, He gave each guest one of the white carnations. When there were only a few left, Leroy, who was standing behind Him, thought, 'Gee, I wish He would turn around and shake hands with me before they are all gone!'

Just as he thought that, 'Abdu'l-Bahá turned, looked at him, and gave him a beautiful red rose that He pulled from His own coat. Leroy was sure that 'Abdu'l-Bahá knew it was him who brought those white carnations. [8]

(8)
Generosity for Everyone

In 'Akká, where the Mansion of Bahjí is, 'Abdu'l-Bahá held a very large feast and He Himself served forty guests. Some people called Bedouins were camping around that area, and they received food as well. Their children came to 'Abdu'l-Bahá and He gave each one of them a coin. The next day, their fathers visited 'Abdu'l-Bahá to thank Him and ask Him for blessings. [9]

'Abdu'l-Bahá's Birthday

When 'Abdu'l-Bahá visited America, a few Baha'is decided to throw a surprise birthday party for Him. First, they baked Him a cake and made sure He did not know about it. Then they went into different taxis and headed towards a park. 'Abdu'l-Bahá was the first to walk into the park when they arrived.

'Abdu'l-Bahá's clothes were Middle Eastern and looked different from what people wore in America. He wore a robe and on top of it a cloak called an "'abá." On His head, he wore "a low-crowned fez, with a fine-linen turban of white wound around the base." [10]

Color portrait of 'Abdu'l-Bahá in Paris, France, October 1911

'A group of young boys gathered around Him and started to laugh. Two or three of them threw stones at Him… Many of the friends hurried towards the Master, but He told them to stay away. The boys came closer to the Master, jeered at Him, and pulled at His clothes. The Master did not become cross. He merely smiled at them radiantly, but the boys continued to behave as before. Then the Master turned towards the friends. "Bring me the cake," He said… Some… said, "But 'Abdu'l-Bahá, the cake is for your birthday." He repeated, "Bring me the cake." A friend uncovered a large sponge cake, with white icing, and gave it to the Master. As soon as the boys had seen the cake they began to calm down, and stared at the cake hungrily. The Master took it in His hands and looked at the cake with pleasure. The boys were now standing quietly around Him. "Bring me a knife," said the Master. A friend brought Him a knife. The Master counted the number of boys who were standing around Him and then cut the cake into the same number of pieces. Each boy eagerly took a piece, ate it with relish, and then ran away happily.' [11]

If you'd like to know more about 'Abdu'l-Bahá, you can visit this website: https://www.bahai.org/abdul-baha/

Even though we haven't seen 'Abdu'l-Bahá in person, we know that He is always with us. Once, 'Abdu'l-Bahá said to a person who expressed his and others' love for Him:

> "I know that you love me, I can see that it is so. I will pray for you that you may be firm and serve in the Cause, becoming a true servant to Bahá'u'lláh. Though I go away I will always be present with you all." [12]

Imagine that you were able to send a letter to 'Abdu'l-Bahá, like many friends used to during His lifetime. What would you write in that letter? What are the things you would like to tell Him? Perhaps you want to make a promise to Him. Bring a pen and paper, with the help of an adult if needed, and write that letter, then keep it somewhere safe and revisit it every once in a while to be reminded of its contents!

A prayer of 'Abdu'l-Bahá for children:

O God! Educate these children. These children are the plants of Thine orchard, the flowers of Thy meadow, the roses of Thy garden. Let Thy rain fall upon them; let the Sun of Reality shine upon them with Thy love. Let Thy breeze refresh them in order that they may be trained, grow and develop, and appear in the utmost beauty. Thou art the Giver. Thou art the Compassionate.[13]

—'Abdu'l Bahá

References:

_____

1 ("The Promulgation of Universal Peace: Talks Delivered by 'Abdu'l-Bahá during His Visit to the United States and Canada in 1912", 2nd. ed. (Wilmette: Bahá'í Publishing Trust, 1982), pp. 52–54) [147]

2 Rabbani, Rúhíyyih Khánum, The priceless Pearl, Baha'i Publishing Trust, 1969

3 Ibid.

4 Ibid.

5 Ibid.

6 Nakhjavani, Violette. The Maxwells of Montreal: Early Years 1870-1922 (The Maxwell of Montreal) . George Ronald. Kindle Edition.

7 Honnold, Annamarie. Vignettes from the Life of 'Abdu'l-Bahá . George Ronald. Kindle Edition.

8 Ibid.

9 Ibid.

10 `Abdu'l-Bahá: Speaking in America, by Allan L. Ward, in World Order, 6:2 (1971) p. 43. Overview of `Abdu'l-Bahá's travels through North America, newspaper coverage of his talks, and first-hand accounts of meeting him

11 Honnold, Annamarie. Vignettes from the Life of 'Abdu'l-Bahá . George Ronald. Kindle Edition.

12 'Abdu'l-Bahá in London, UK Bahá'í Publishing Trust, 1982, p. 112.

13 https://www.bahai.org/library/authoritative-texts/prayers/bahai-prayers/3#579021329

All the photographed images are from this website: https://media.bahai.org/

Other Bahá'í books by Alhan Rahimi:

In 1912, 'Abdu'l-Bahá visited New York. This story is about an encounter He had with a child who was racially different from the group of children who met with Him.

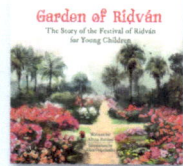
A nightingale tells us about the garden he lived in and the twelve joyful days that we celebrate today as the Festival of Riḍván

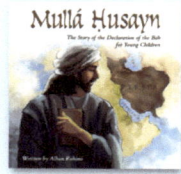
Mullá Ḥusayn was the first believer in the Báb. This story tries to demonstrate his endeavour to reach to his heart's desire through prayer and hard work.

In 1819, a unique Child was born. The moon remembers His birth and childhood. This book is about the Báb's childhood, written in simple language for young children.

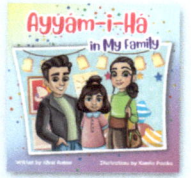
This story shows a family's celebration of Ayyám-i-Há. In it, Maya shares what her family does during this time of year.

Alice tells us about her family's celebration of Naw-Rúz, the Bahá'í New Year.